The A.D.D.
Book for Kids

The A.D.D. Book for Kids

Written by **Shelley Rotner** and **Sheila Kelly, Ed.D.**

Photographs by **Shelley Rotner**

The Millbrook Press M Brookfield, Connecticut

Note for Parents and Teachers

The *Diagnostic and Statistical Manual of Mental Disorders* (fourth edition) defines Attention-Deficit/Hyperactivity Disorder as a behavior disorder characterized by an inability to give close or sustained attention to a task, an inability to organize and plan, and a tendency to forgetfulness and to making careless mistakes. It occurs in three to five percent of children, more frequently in boys than in girls, and symptoms persist into adulthood with varying degrees of intensity.

The disorder, commonly known as ADD (although we call it A.D.D. in the text of this book in order to avoid confusion on the part of youngsters with the word "add"), may or may not involve the "on the go" behavior generally described as hyperactivity, and the degree of impulsivity exhibited may vary. Those individuals who experience the condition without hyperactivity are often labeled lazy or called daydreamers.

In his book, *Driven to Distraction*, which he wrote with Dr. John Ratey, Dr. Ned Hallowell tells of his personal experience upon learning that he had ADD. He says it made him realize "I wasn't all the names I had been called in grade school—a daydreamer, lazy, an underachiever, a spaceshot— and I didn't have some repressed, unconscious conflict." In fact, the cause of ADD has nothing to do with intelligence or motivation. People with ADD have been misdiagnosed and misunderstood for years.

There is no lab test for Attention Deficit Disorder. Diagnosis is based on systematic observation of specific behaviors and careful history taking. However, after decades of research, neuroscientists have been able to establish that attention disorders are biologically based.

In November 1990 a team led by Dr. Alan Zametkin at the National Institutes of Mental Health published a landmark study in *The New England Journal of Medicine*. The article described essential differences in the brain metabolism of individuals with Attention-Deficit/Hyperactivity Disorder and those who did not exhibit symptoms of the disorder. This supported clinicians' understanding of attention problems as neurochemically based and often able to be alleviated by medication. Research continues into the ways that medication can assist in the management of this disorder.

In 1991 the U.S. Department of Education officially recognized ADD as a condition that interferes with learning and that warrants special intervention. Parents and professionals across the country had lobbied for such understanding and welcomed it, but there are still children with varying degrees of ADD who feel misunderstood. They are not comfortable speaking about their condition in the way children with asthma or diabetes may be. We hope this book will make it easier for all children to talk about ADD among themselves and with their families and teachers. We hope it will help those living with ADD to explain it to others and (for those children suffering from it) to feel proud of their successes.

SHEILA M. KELLY, Ed.D.

Have you heard of a condition
that creates problems for some kids?

Doctors call it **Attention Deficit Disorder** or **A.D.D.**

Kids with this condition can tell us about it.

"It can be
different
for each one
of us."

Sometimes it's hard to pay attention.

"My coach is always hollering at me."

"I think of
other things."

Sometimes it's hard to **stop and think.**

"And I just blurt things out."

Sometimes it's hard to keep track of things.

Lost and Found

"It's embarrassing to lose your stuff."

Sometimes it's hard to stay with a job until you finish . . . and **you're often late.**

Getting help from parents, teachers . . .

. . . and friends is really important.

Rachel's teacher gives her
one assignment at a time.

"Before I had my tutor I never handed work in on time."

Amanda's teacher finds her a quiet work corner.

Elizabeth's mom made a
Job Chart at home.

Doctors say,

"A.D.D. is not your fault.

It doesn't mean you're not smart."

"You can learn to manage it, though
it doesn't go away."

George gets **medicine that helps.**

When your family and friends
understand . . .

. . . things get easier, you feel better . . .

. . . and you succeed.